To

_____

From

_____

Christmas Teas
OF COMFORT AND JOY

EMILIE BARNES *Paintings by* SUSAN RIOS

HARVEST HOUSE PUBLISHERS

EUGENE, OREGON

Christmas Teas of Comfort and Joy

Text Copyright © 1999 by Harvest House Publishers
Art Copyright © 2008 by Susan Rios

Published by Harvest House Publishers
Eugene, Oregon 97402
www.harvesthousepublishers.com

ISBN-13: 978-0-7369-2229-6
ISBN-10: 0-7369-2229-6

Text is excerpted from *The Twelve Teas® of Christmas*

Original artwork by Susan Rios. For more information regarding artwork featured in this book, please contact:

Susan Rios Editions
263 West Olive Ave., #275
Burbank, California 91502
(818) 571-7134 www.susanrioseditions.com

Design and production by Garborg Design Works, Savage, Minnesota

Scripture quotations are taken from the HOLY BIBLE, NEW INTERNATIONAL VERSION®. NIV®. Copyright©1973, 1978, 1984 by the International Bible Society. Used by permission of Zondervan. All rights reserved.

Printed in the United States of America

08 09 10 11 12 13 14 15 / LT / 10 9 8 7 6 5 4 3

Contents

For SANTA

Family Traditions

BUILDING TRADITION WHILE SPENDING HOLIDAY TIME TOGETHER

You're invited to a togetherness tea party full of fun, games, treats, and hugs—a party just for our family!

When I think of Christmas, I think of family. During the Christmas season, families need to make a place in their lives for the legacy of sharing. This is the time when memories are made, old traditions are carried out, and new traditions are created. Perhaps Dad always reads *A Child's Christmas in Wales* on Christmas Eve, or everyone gathers in the family room to watch *It's a Wonderful Life* the day after Thanksgiving. Maybe you and your children bundle up in your warmest attire and head into the mountains to get your Christmas tree on the first weekend in December. Or perhaps you're like a lot of families, who would love to start forming and sharing traditions but, in the midst of the gift shopping and the card writing and the goodie baking, haven't quite arrived at that point.

Why not start a tradition of sharing a Family Traditions tea party? Children get excited about tea parties too! After all, what child doesn't love playing dress up, receiving a colorful party invitation, playing games, and eating yummy treats? A family tea provides a time for parents and children to come together in an afternoon or evening of fun. You'll share in the anticipation of the season, talk about the meaning of Christmas, and build tradition.

Send Family Traditions tea party invitations to your children and your spouse! You can slip them under their door, hide them with the day's letters, or even send them in the "real" mail. If you're single, you can "adopt" some children of your own—your nieces and nephews, the kids down the street, a few of the grade-schoolers at your church. Try to keep it cozy. And enjoy your hearty cup of togetherness tea!

Menu for a Family Traditions Tea Party

FRUIT SALSA • ASSORTED CHEESES •
CHRISTMAS TREE BREAD • HAM-FILLED SANDWICH SPREAD

RECIPES

Fruit Salsa

2 medium Granny Smith apples
1½ cups fresh strawberries
1 kiwi
1 small orange
2 tablespoons brown sugar
2 tablespoons apple jelly

Peel, core, and chop apples. Hull strawberries and slice. Peel, core, and chop kiwi. Grate 2 tablespoons orange zest, squeeze rest of orange to equal ¼ cup of juice. Stir all of the above with brown sugar and apple jelly in a bowl. Terrific on bread and muffins!

Christmas Tree Bread

2 packages active dry yeast
½ cup warm water
1¼ cups buttermilk
½ cup sugar
½ cup margarine, softened
2 eggs
2 teaspoons baking powder
2 teaspoons salt
5½ cups flour

Dissolve yeast in warm water in large mixing bowl. Add buttermilk, sugar, margarine, eggs, baking powder, salt, and 2½ cups flour. Beat on low speed, scraping bowl constantly, for 30 seconds. Beat on medium speed, scraping bowl occasionally, for 2 minutes. Stir in remaining flour. Dough will be soft and slightly sticky. Turn dough onto well-floured surface; knead until smooth and elastic, about 5 minutes. Divide dough in half (to form two trees); shape one half at a time into seventeen 2-inch balls. Form tree shape with balls in rows of 5, 4, 3, 2, 1 on lightly greased cookie sheet. Roll remaining 2 balls together for trunk of tree. Cover; let rise in warm place for 1 hour. Bake at 350 degrees until golden brown, 20-25 minutes. Remove from cookie sheet and cool.

Beat 2 cups powdered sugar, 2-3 tablespoons water or milk, and 1 teaspoon vanilla until smooth. Decorate trees with frosting. Trim with candied fruit.

Ham-Filled Sandwich Spread

½ pound cooked ham
1 large dill pickle
4 hard-cooked eggs
2 teaspoons mustard
3 tablespoons mayonnaise
Salt and pepper to taste

Combine ham, pickle, eggs, and mustard in food processor. Moisten with mayonnaise. Season with salt and pepper.

Did You Know...?

It was Queen Victoria's influence that allowed children to play more and work less. The queen held parties at Christmastime especially for children, encouraging them to take part in the festivity of the season.

A Word About Tea

While children should not drink caffeinated beverages, herbal teas are both yummy and good for little ones. Lavender tea can calm cranky youngsters. Chamomile, one of the best-loved herbal teas, contains a completely natural sedative that helps soothe you to sleep. If you're using loose tea, simply measure two teaspoons of tea leaves per four-cup pot. Steep twenty minutes, then strain well. And enjoy a family tradition of togetherness!

READYING THE ROOMS

A wonderful way to build tradition *and* decorate your house for the holidays is to devote a portion of your family time to getting and trimming the Christmas tree. If you haven't yet purchased your tree, take the whole family to a tree farm or lot to pick one out. The trip will become a ritual in itself!

While in search of a tree, share the story of the origins of this now-familiar symbol of Christmas. Its story comes to us from Germany, where the theologian Martin Luther cut and decorated the first Christmas tree for his children in 1535. According to legend, Luther was walking home through the woods one Christmas Eve under the bright, starry sky, contemplating the wonder and beauty of the evening and wishing he could somehow capture the moment to share with his children. An image of a tall evergreen tree sparkling with candlelight popped into his mind, and on his way he found a tree just the right size. He cut it down, carried it home, and decorated it. And, just as he'd imagined, his children were overjoyed. In 1841, the custom began in England when Prince Albert had a Christmas tree set up in Windsor Castle especially for his wife, Queen Victoria, and their children. As you can see, the putting up of the Christmas tree is certainly a family affair!

Once you've selected your tree, reward yourself with a hearty tea before the trimming begins. If your tree is already up, you could take some time to make a few special ornaments or get a roaring fire going while you are untangling outdoor lights or sorting through Christmas decorations.

For a tree rich in memories, display all the ornaments your family has collected over the years. And be sure to let the children hang some of the ornaments. Mom might want to hang all of the fragile silver balls, or Dad could be in charge of the lights. But certainly let the little ones help. They'll be proud of how they, too, have made the tree pretty!

Once you're finished decorating the tree, turn off all the lights and gather round to admire your family's creation. Pour cups of herbal tea or cocoa and then snuggle up together on the sofa to sing Christmas carols, tell stories, or reminisce about past Christmases as you celebrate the warmth of togetherness. You might decide to come together to admire the tree *every* evening of December!

A Teddy Bear for the Tree

For each bear, you'll need:

One Christmas ball ornament
Four ½-inch pom-poms
Three ¼-inch pom-poms
One 2-inch pom-pom
One pair googly eyes
Scrap of red felt
Hot glue gun and glue sticks

Start by gluing the 2-inch pom-pom on top of the ball ornament, just in front of the hanger, to form the bear's head. Next make the ears by gluing two of the ¼-inch pom-poms to the top of the head. Then glue the third ¼-inch pom- *pom to the center of the face—that's the nose! Add your googly eyes above the nose, cut a wide grin from the red felt, and glue it underneath the nose. Now you're ready to form the body! Glue all four ½-inch pom-poms to the ornament to form four legs. You can decorate the bear's tummy—write your name on it, jot a Christmas greeting, or draw a picture—with three-dimensional paint. You can add additional pom-poms to make long bunny ears, or cut out pointed pieces of felt to make a cat too.*

A Season of Anticipation

It's fun to create your own family Advent calendar. Here are three ideas for a season of anticipation:

• **Open the Door:** Draw a Christmas scene on a sheet of construction paper, and sketch 25 little doors on it. Mark the doors 1-25, then cut three sides so they open and close just like a real door would. Now place this sheet of paper over another sheet of paper. Draw a picture or write a Christmas saying behind every door. Glue the first sheet (the one with the doors) over the second sheet (the one with the pictures or sayings). If the doors don't stay closed, you can use small pieces of tape.

• **A Season of Sweets:** Choose 25 pieces of individually wrapped hard candies. Tie each candy to a piece of twine, a strand of red or green yarn, or a thin piece of torn Christmas fabric. Then hang all the strings of candy on a coat hanger, a drapery rod, or even on the Christmas tree. Take turns enjoying a piece of candy every day. As the candy supply diminishes, Christmas is getting closer!

• **Christmas Chain:** Make a paper chain out of red and green construction paper. Before you connect and glue the pieces in the chain, number them 1-25. You can also write a little message, a part of the Christmas story, or the promise for a small treat on each one. Break off a piece of the chain every day of Advent.

Customs of Christmas

A Christmas tradition I've long cherished is the tradition of the Advent calendar. Advent is the four-week period prior to Christmas that serves as a time of preparing the heart and the spirit for the coming of the Christ child. Many people celebrate Advent by purchasing or making an Advent calendar—a calendar that contains a door for each of the twenty-four days before Christmas that, when opened, reveals a picture or a small treat. On the twenty-fifth day, the door generally opens to reveal a Nativity scene. Others celebrate the season of Advent by lighting the candles of the Advent wreath each night and saying a prayer. The evergreens in the Advent wreath symbolize life and growth; the shape of the wreath, a circle, is a sign of eternity without end; and the lighted candles stand for the presence of God.

Your family might choose to celebrate Advent by doing a special Christmas activity every day. At the beginning of the month, write down twenty-four ways to celebrate the season on small slips of paper. Then place the slips into a decorated jar. Each day, take turns drawing an idea from your Advent jar. By thinking of the activities and doing them together, you're sure to create even more family traditions!

The rooms were very still while the pages were softly turned and the winter sunshine crept in to touch the bright heads and serious faces with a Christmas greeting.

—Louisa May Alcott, *Little Women*

2
Welcome Friends

STARTING OFF THE HOLIDAY SEASON
WITH A HEART FULL OF WELCOME

*You are invited to begin the Christmas season with a
very special tea party given in celebration of our friendship.*

Every year I love to see the signs point to winter's approach—spirited late-afternoon windstorms that send fiery orange-and-yellow leaves scurrying off the trees, the transition from breezy cotton to cozy flannel sheets, wool sweaters, and warm coats brought forth from trunks and drawers. There's an excitement that permeates the chill in the air, a growing feeling of anticipation, a heightened expectation of things yet to come. Christmas is on the way!

During the Christmas season, we celebrate all that is good. We send others our most sincere wishes of peace, joy, and love. From giving gifts to decorating our homes to offering extra smiles and words of encouragement, we're helping add to the feeling of goodwill that embraces the holiday season. In our interaction with those around us—family both immediate and extended, friends new and old, coworkers and members of the small groups to which we belong—we are given one opportunity after another to make someone else's Christmas a little more meaningful, a little more memorable, a little more beautiful.

One of the best ways to start the season off in festive fashion is by inviting a group of special people to begin the celebration with you—a few close friends, a study group, your sisters, the people in your department at work. A Welcome Friends tea party is a celebration just perfect for the occasion. In a salute to both companionship and Christmas, a Welcome Friends tea party helps you kick off the holidays on a festive note, preparing your heart and your home for the days of joy to come.

Menu for a Welcome Friends Tea Party

NUT BREAD WITH THREE-APPLE BUTTER • TUNA PINWHEELS
CRANBERRY STREUSEL CAKE • BEST-TASTING BROWNIES

RECIPES

Three-Apple Butter

1 pound unsalted sweet butter
1 Granny Smith apple, quartered with core and skin
1 Winesap apple, quartered with core and skin
1 Macon apple, quartered with core and skin

(You may use any combination of apples, as long as some are tart and some are sweet.)

Place all ingredients in a heavy 4-quart saucepan. Cook 30 minutes over medium-low heat, lowering heat as apples cook and stirring occasionally. Force mixture through a sieve or stainless steel strainer. Cool, cover saucepan, and refrigerate. Makes 3 cups.

Tuna Pinwheels

1-pound loaf of unsliced, day-old white
    bread (fresh-baked will be difficult to cut)
½ cup unsalted butter, room temperature
Your favorite tuna salad

*Neatly cut off all crust from loaf of bread. Cut
lengthwise into very thin slices. Lightly spread
butter to edges of one side. Spread buttered slice
with tuna salad. Roll up lengthwise, jelly roll-
style. Wrap in foil. Repeat until loaf is finished.
(You should have about 6 rolls.) Refrigerate
for at least an hour; butter will harden and
hold rolls together. Before serving, cut each roll
cross-wise into about 5 slices. Makes about 30
pinwheels.*

Cranberry Streusel Cake

Streusel Mixture:

¾ cup packed light brown sugar
1 teaspoon cinnamon
¼ cup flour
¼ cup butter or margarine

*In a small bowl, cut and mix together above
ingredients, then set aside.*

Did You Know...?

The name "Christmas" comes from the Latin
"Christes Masse" of Christ's Mass. It grew
out of the Roman Catholic feast day by that
name in approximately AD 100.

Cake Mixture:

½ cup butter or margarine
2 eggs
1 cup sour cream
1 cup sugar
1 teaspoon vanilla

*Beat cake ingredients together in large bowl.
Gradually add to the above mixture the
following dry ingredients:*

2 cups flour
1 teaspoon baking soda
1 teaspoon baking powder
½ teaspoon salt

*Wash 1 bag of fresh or frozen cranberries
and set aside. Preheat oven to 350 degrees.
Grease an angel food cake pan. Spread half
of cake mixture into pan, followed by half of
streusel mixture and half of cranberries. Repeat
with other half batter, then cranberries, then
streusel. Bake 1-1½ hours.*

Best-Tasting Brownies

1 family-size package Duncan Hines fudge
  brownie mix with chocolate syrup
2 large eggs
2 teaspoons water
¼ cup oil
1 cup chocolate chips
1 cup chopped walnuts
1 cup white mini marshmallows

*Combine all ingredients. Spread in 9 x 13 pan.
Bake at 350 degrees for 30 minutes.*

A Word About Tea

Raise a cup of tea as a toast to good health! Tea drinking is a delightful habit to cultivate. Not only does the ceremony of teatime lift spirits, the health benefits are yours to enjoy as well! Tea helps relieve fatigue, lift the spirits, and stimulate the mind. A cup of tea contains zero calories (add approximately 40 for a cup taken with milk and sugar), yet provides you with several of the complex vitamins.

READYING THE ROOMS

To help get yourself—as well as your guests—in the Christmas spirit, pull out your boxes of holiday decorations, jot down a list of the main areas of your house, inside and out, you'd like to dress up for the holidays. If possible, have a Welcome Friends tea party on the very first day of December. Your guests will come away from your party inspired to decorate their own homes with cheery lights and welcoming wreaths.

We have the Victorians to thank for the fanciful ornaments of Christmas—candy canes, nutcrackers and gingerbread men, glittering glass balls, and romantic sprigs of mistletoe. Not until the middle of the nineteenth century did many of the familiar Christmas decorations become common in our country.

Even if you have no tree, you can fill your home with the sights and smells of Christmas. Head to a nearby garden store or into the great outdoors to pick up branches of evergreen, balsam, or juniper. Outline mirrors with the fragrant branches, arrange them on mantels and windowsills, on tabletops and bookshelves. It's pretty to add small, simple

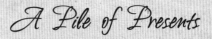

A Pile of Presents

Not all Christmas packages need to be wrapped up in paper. Gather up your decorative pillows and gift-wrap them for the holidays. Choose some satin or organdy ribbon (three inches is a good width) in colors that match your pillows. Tie the ribbon onto the pillows, complete with cheery bows, and return them to their respective places, properly dressed in Christmas finery!

ornaments—gold or silver balls, for instance—for a touch of merriment. Or showcase your holiday collectibles in among the branches—snow villages, collections of angels, and, of course, Christmas teacups!

For a tea party held in the dining room, weave Christmas-colored ribbons through or hang small stockings on chairbacks. Wrap small boxes in Christmas paper and use them as place cards, writing each guest's name on a tag. (You can even put a small gift inside—a chocolate truffle, a little box of tea, a handmade ornament.)

To make your Welcome Friends tea party *really* seem British, hold it in your living room. (You can call it the "drawing room" just for fun.) Top a high, round table with a long skirt to make an official tea table, and pull chairs and sofas into a cozy circle facing the fireplace and each other. Turn off the overhead lights, relying only on lamplight and the fire to provide a soft, intimate glow. And dress the furniture in the room for Christmas using merry red or green slipcovers and pillow covers.

With a few more touches—indoor wreaths and garlands, bows tied on candlesticks and plenty of candles in seasonal colors and scents set about, cozy throws and cheery table runners, a Nativity scene or a special Advent calendar, a gathering of family photos decorated with bows and greens—your home will be brimming with welcome and good cheer!

CUSTOMS OF CHRISTMAS

One of our first holiday tasks is the writing and sending of Christmas cards. The custom began in Great Britain around 1840 with the advent of the "Penny Post"—the first public postal delivery system. Legend tells that a procrastinating Englishman named Henry Cole actually started the tradition. In 1843, he found himself behind in his correspondence with friends and wanted to set things right with a cheery Christmas note to end the year. His resourceful idea led to a mass marketing of holiday cards, particularly after 1860 as printing methods improved. In Britain, sending season's greetings jumped in popularity when a card could be posted in an unsealed envelope for just one half-penny—half the price of a regular letter. In 1865, Bostonian Louis Prang printed and sold the first Christmas card in the United States. The images and message have remained fairly constant throughout the years—pictures showing the Christmas story or other seasonal scenes along with wishes of a merry Christmas and a happy new year.

Include your Welcome Friends tea invitations along with your Christmas cards if you send them out early enough, or you can even devote a portion of your tea party to Christmas card writing if you're gathering together with a group of like-minded and time-pressed friends! Provide colorful pens, festive rubber stamps, and holiday music for a relaxing time of catching up family and friends on the year's happenings.

What is the Christmas spirit?
It is the spirit which brings a
smile to the lips and tenderness to
the heart; it is the spirit which
warms one into friendship with all
the world, which impels one to
hold out the hand of fellowship
to every man and woman.

—ANONYMOUS

Films to Get You in the Festive Spirit

March of the Wooden Soldiers, starring Laurel and Hardy (1934)

Holiday Inn, starring Fred Astaire and Bing Crosby (1942)

It's a Wonderful Life, starring Jimmy Stewart, Lionel Barrymore, and Donna Reed (1946)

Miracle on 34th Street, starring Natalie Wood and Maureen O'Hara (1947)

The Bishop's Wife, starring Cary Grant, David Niven, and Loretta Young (1947)

White Christmas, starring Danny Kaye and Bing Crosby (1954)

The Nutcracker, (any professional ballet or ice adaptation)

3

A-Caroling We Go

SPREADING THE MESSAGE OF THE SEASON THROUGH SONG

*Here we come a-caroling! We'll stroll through the neighborhood singing
and then return to my house for food and conversation.*

A cheery group of Christmas carolers at my door always brings a smile to my face and joy to my heart. Caroling is such an old-fashioned, homey way of spreading the good news of the season. In modern-day America, a group of Christmas carolers serenading your home is a fairly uncommon occurrence. Most of us rely on our CD players and radios to provide us with holiday music. But there's just something about a group of carolers that outshines even the best recording of "Silent Night" or "The Coventry Carol." Dressed in warm coats and scarves, making their way from house to house with laughter and conversation, these groups of singing angels lend a neighborly caring to big-city streets and country roads alike. Voices young and old, high and low, blend together in a familiar chorus to bring a touch of neighborly kindness and caring to the evening.

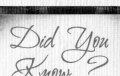

When you're preparing for your A-Caroling We Go tea party, be sure to prepare enough extra food to go around. This is the sort of event where a few additional people show up and join the festivities. And they're always welcome to do so! After all, this tea party is about sharing—sharing your time and your happiness and your home with others.

In your invitations, encourage all the carolers to bring lanterns or flashlights and to bundle up, especially if snow or cold weather is in the forecast. Depending on what time you decide to carol, you can serve tea either before or after the singing. A party around dinnertime calls for an early, hearty tea so your carolers will be well fortified to sing their best. And a celebration later in the evening can conclude with hot tea and cookies or cakes. Because your guests will be giving to others, you can reward them by giving something to them!

Christmas Eve was a night of song that wrapped itself about you like a shawl. But it warmed more than your body. It warmed your heart...filled it, too, with a melody that would last forever.

—BESS STREETER ALDRICH

Menu for an A-Caroling We Go Tea Party

RECIPES

Seafood Butter

1 cup cooked shrimp or lobster
¼ pound butter
½ teaspoon lemon juice
Pepper to taste

Combine all ingredients into blender. Blend on high until spreadable. Chill before serving. Serve on slices of a mini pumpernickel loaf or other flavorful bread.

Sweet Poppy Seed Bread

1 box yellow cake mix
Small box vanilla pudding mix
5 eggs
½ cup oil
½ cup water
½ cup orange juice
1 tablespoon almond extract
½ cup poppy seeds

Combine all ingredients. Bake at 325 degrees for 50 minutes in greased loaf pan. Makes two loaves.

Nut Gem Cookies

1 cup butter
4 tablespoons sugar
2 tablespoons milk
2 teaspoons rum extract
2 cups flour
1 cup chopped walnuts

Mix, chill, and roll into small balls. Bake at 300 degrees for 15 minutes. Roll in powdered sugar after balls are slightly cooled.

Peanut Brittle

1 cup peanuts
1 cup sugar
⅛ teaspoon salt
½ cup white corn syrup
1 teaspoon butter
1 teaspoon vanilla
1 teaspoon baking soda

Stir peanuts, sugar, and salt; add syrup in 1½-quart glass bowl. Microwave on high 7-8 minutes; stir well after 4 minutes. At end of 7-8 minutes, add butter and vanilla. Blend well. Return to microwave and cook on high 1-2 minutes more. Remove from oven and add baking soda. Stir until light and foamy. Pour immediately onto greased cookie sheet. Cool 30-60 minutes. Break into pieces and store in airtight container.

READYING THE ROOMS

To prepare for an A-Caroling We Go tea party, make sure your home is cozy and clean inside, with the tea table set and chairs and sofas plumped up and made inviting with plush pillows and festive throws. The main part of your party, however, will be held out-of-doors. In essence, you're bringing the celebration to the homes at which you carol. While some of your neighbors might invite you in to warm your hands and have something toasty to drink, for the most part you and your guests will be sharing your hospitality with them. So think of yourself as having two sets of guests—the guests you invite to go caroling with you and the guests to whom you sing!

You can purchase inexpensive songbooks or pages of sheet music at a local music store to prepare for the caroling. Another good idea is to borrow some hymnbooks from your church, or print pages of Christmas carols off of the Internet. Or ask your guests to bring favorite music of their own. You might even want to run through a few songs with everyone before leaving the house to spark everyone's Christmas cheer.

Take that same Christmas spirit to your neighborhood. Along with the gift of song, it's fun to give away other presents while caroling. Make up plates of cookies, baskets of bread, or bags of "beanbag" soup mix (see next page) to leave at each house. If your caroling group includes several other bakers, invite them to contribute cookies or breads to the celebration. Add a bow and a card to each package and your gift is complete. By delivering the goodies personally, you'll get to visit elderly people who often stay indoors and neighbors who aren't at home very much.

Most of all, sing loudly, put a smile on your face, and wish everyone you pass a spirited "Merry Christmas!"

The Story of "Silent Night"

There's a charming story behind the favorite carol "Silent Night." It was December 23, 1818, and the setting was the village of Oberndorf, Austria. Franz Gruber, a church organist, and Father Mohr, the priest, discovered a hole gnawed by a mouse in the leather bellows of the church organ. The thought of a Christmas service with no music saddened them both, but there was no way to fix the organ. Franz, thinking quickly, handed the priest a simple poem he had written and asked Father Mohr to set the words to music. On Christmas Eve, Father Mohr strummed his guitar while a choir of twelve boys and girls sang in clear, innocent voices the words to "Silent Night," filling the air with quiet reverence.

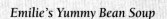

Emilie's Yummy Bean Soup

This is the recipe I like to include with my gifts of "beanbag" soup.

*1 package of gift beans
1 large onion, chopped
1 29-ounce can crushed tomatoes
1 clove crushed garlic
Juice of 1 lemon
Salt and pepper to taste

Wash beans thoroughly and place in large pot. Add enough water to cover beans by two inches. Boil two minutes and let stand one hour. Drain and add two quarts of water and ½ pound of ham or ham hocks and simmer 1½ to 2 hours, covered. Add the rest of the ingredients and simmer 30 minutes or until beans are tender. Makes 10 to 12 big servings.

* To make enough soup mix for eight gift bags with 2½ cups of beans for each bag, I combine 2 cups of each of the following types of beans in a large container–black beans, pinto beans, pearl barley, lima beans, lentils, butter beans or large limas, navy beans, split green peas, red beans, and Great Northern beans. (You may use any combination.) Divide the mixture into bags, add a cute tag and a recipe card, and your thoughtful gift will feed many!

Carolers' Wassail Bowl

My Christmas wassail recipe is sure to reward an enthusiastic group of carolers!

1 gallon apple cider
1 large can pineapple juice
1 cup orange spice herb tea
1 tablespoon whole cloves
1 tablespoon whole allspice
2 cinnamon sticks
Square piece of muslin cloth
Small piece of string

Mix the juices together in a big pot or crockery pot. Put the spices in the middle of a small square of muslin cloth and tie with a string into a little bundle. Put the spice bag in the pot and let the whole thing simmer 4 to 8 hours. Add water if the wassail gets too strong.

CUSTOMS OF CHRISTMAS

Did you know that not all songs we sing at Christmastime are truly carols? Many centuries ago, a carol was a dance accompanied by a merry song. The meaning gradually changed to include the song itself—a joyful tune that anyone could sing. The word "caroling" means "celebrating in song."

During the Middle Ages, groups of men and boys roamed the streets of London in search of food or money. The groups traveled from house to house, singing ancient hymns and spreading holiday spirit in exchange for a bit of food or a few coins. Later in the day, the "waifs" would make their rounds. They were carolers, generally children, who sang and danced.

Many ancient carols were composed to retell the Christmas story, long before people had access to books or sheets of music. Years later, great musicians and theologians composed some of the carols we now consider classics. Martin Luther penned the words to "Away in a Manger," Mendelssohn composed "Hark! The Herald Angels Sing," and Handel wrote "Joy to the World" along with what is widely regarded as his masterpiece, *Messiah*.

In Australia, a popular custom is "Carols by Candlelight," a communal outdoor sing-along. When darkness falls, groups as small as five or as large as fifty thousand join together to sing Christmas songs while holding candles or torches. Norman Banks of Melbourne is credited with beginning this tradition in 1937. He came up with the idea after he saw an old widow holding a single candle and singing along with her radio. It's a joyous tradition.

Suddenly a great company of the heavenly host appeared with the angel, praising God and saying, "Glory to God in the highest, and on earth peace to men on whom his favor rests."

—THE GOSPEL OF LUKE

4
Old-Fashioned Fun

ENJOYING BEST-LOVED RITUALS AND OLD-FASHIONED HOLIDAY FUN

Step back in time and celebrate Christmas the old-fashioned way with traditional food, games, and fun!

Perhaps the one word we link with Christmas more than any other is "tradition." We carry boxes full of holiday decorations down from the attic or in from the garage, unpacking them with glee and exclaiming over forgotten ornaments or favorite table runners. That's tradition. Many of us bring our Christmas CDs to the forefront on the first day of December, playing exclusively seasonal music to warm our days. That's tradition. We outline our rooftops with glittering lights, get out our most festive cookie cutters, or head downtown for an evening of holiday shopping. Those, too, are traditions.

Traditions make us feel good, giving us a sense of belonging to our family and to our community, and providing an anchor for the days of joy to come. One fun way to celebrate the customs of Christmas is to hold an Old-Fashioned Fun tea party, one with an

Old World flair. Focus on the rustic, the simple, and the homemade. You'll not only create a quaint, old-fashioned feel, but you'll also find pleasure in the simple things of the season.

Read historical novels or American classics to put you in the old-fashioned spirit of things. Laura Ingalls Wilder's Little House books are highly recommended, as is anything by Midwestern writer Willa Cather. You can also search specialty music stores for regional recordings of traditional music. Take advantage of the opportunity to learn a little more about the area in which you live or the part of the country where your ancestors settled. And then host a tea party that highlights what you discover.

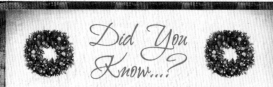

Did You Know...?

According to legend, the candy cane was invented by an English candy maker in the seventeenth century. The government did not let the people celebrate Christmas at that time, so the candy maker fashioned a sweet, hard candy shaped like a shepherd's crook as a secret symbol of the Christmas story. The white represented purity and the red represented life. Now, of course, Christmas is celebrated throughout the world, and candy canes are a familiar part of the holidays.

Menu for an Old-Fashioned Fun Tea Party

WATERCRESS SANDWICHES • DATE-NUT BARS
CHRISTMAS CLOVER COOKIES • MIXED FRUIT MEDLEY

RECIPES

Watercress Sandwiches

Butter white or rye bread and fill with watercress leaves. Cut into squares, arrange on a plate, and garnish with watercress.

Date-Nut Bars

1 cup butter, melted
1 cup white sugar
1 cup brown sugar
4 eggs
1 teaspoon vanilla
15 ounces chopped dates
2 cups chopped walnuts
1½ cups flour, sifted
1 teaspoon baking powder

Mix butter and sugar. Add eggs and vanilla. Stir in dates and nuts. Fold in flour and baking powder. Spread on greased 9 x 13 pan. Bake at 350 degrees for 30 minutes. Cool and cut into squares. Roll in powdered sugar.

Christmas Clover Cookies

1 cup shortening
2⅔ cups flour
½ cup white sugar
2 teaspoons cream of tartar
½ cup brown sugar
1 teaspoon baking soda
1 egg
Food coloring
3 teaspoons milk
Raisins or nuts
2 teaspoons vanilla

Mix shortening, sugars, eggs, milk, and vanilla. Add sifted dry ingredients. Divide dough into 3 parts and put into separate bowls. Add green food coloring to one bowl, red to another, and leave the third plain. Chill dough 1 hour. With each color, roll small amount of dough in hand and lay one of each color together on a cookie sheet in the form of a cloverleaf. Put raisins or nuts in center. Bake in preheated oven at 350 degrees until done.

READYING THE ROOMS

In Early American times, holiday decorating was much simpler than it is today. Families did not have department stores or mail order catalogs—not to mention Internet shopping! When you're decorating for your Old-Fashioned Fun tea party, use the simplest of items that can readily be found in nature. Gather up an armful of pine branches to line a mantel, and add some color with just a few oranges tucked into the greenery.

To decorate your tree, weave strings of popcorn and cranberries or paper chains throughout the branches. Children will enjoy making chains out of colorful construction paper. Set aside the necessary supplies and prepare to offer as much assistance as needed. Tell stories by the fire or take turns writing Christmas cards while making the strings. Did you know that popcorn strings have long been used in the United States? When the European settlers arrived on the continent, they found people adorning statues and even themselves with strands of popcorn!

In the Northeastern woods, you might find decorations of bayberry and pine boughs accented with rose hips throughout a frontier cabin. Families would have brought Christmas trees home from the woods on sleds. The tree would be trimmed with strings of popcorn and cranberries, popcorn balls (to be eaten later), little presents, and candles in tin holders (our electric lights are thankfully much safer). The table would be simply decorated with a plain cloth made of muslin or paper, several candles in sturdy pewter candlesticks, and a few branches of greenery.

If you were growing up in the woods of the American frontier, a winter storm blowing fiercely outside was typical on Christmas Eve. While the wind whistled and fat snowflakes piled up on the ground, families stayed warm and cozy indoors by the fire where stockings were hanging. Most holiday celebrations in frontier cabins were a blend of Old World customs and New World creativity.

Proper entertainment is a consideration when you're planning your Old-Fashioned Fun tea party. Remember that the early Americans didn't watch television programs or rent movies. Activities that involve everyone and promote conversation are more fun, anyway. Old-time games include hide the thimble, blindman's bluff, and definitions (similar to the current dictionary board game, Balderdash). Or get out your favorite board games and chess and checkers sets. If your gathering is large, set out several card tables around the house and encourage your guests to sit down and partake in some friendly competition.

What traditions of your own can you invent to make Christmas extra special in your household? Perhaps you can dream up an original character who comes to visit at your Old-Fashioned Fun tea. Maybe Dad gets up on the roof and imitates the sound of reindeer hooves for all to hear. Or a mysterious visitor knocks on the door just before teatime and deposits a load of Christmas cookies and candy canes on the front doorstep. With just a little bit of imagination, you too can have a meaningful Old-Fashioned Fun tea party.

All you need for an evening of traditional good cheer is a simple yet abundant supply of goodies, plenty of hot chocolate, eggnog, and tea, a few modest games and ideas, and a heart full of welcome. Your tea party will become something that all of your guests look forward to year after year.

CUSTOMS OF CHRISTMAS

Of all traditional holiday foods, gingerbread is among the most delightful. Stories like "Hansel and Gretel" and "The Gingerbread Man" lend a whimsical touch to the easy-to-make cookie, and ornate gingerbread houses give gingerbread an air of elegance. Gingerbread has a long history. Its origins go all the way back to the eleventh century, when Crusaders returning from the Middle East came back with a new spice called "ginger." Shortly afterward, many different types of gingerbread sprung up throughout Western Europe—some light and some dark, some sweet and some spiced, some moist and some dry.

Gingerbread was actually not called gingerbread until the fifteenth century, when it

A Word About Tea

Tea bags were invented quite by accident in 1904 by a New York tea merchant. Instead of sending samples of tea to his customers in standard tea tins, the innovative merchant came up with the idea of packaging them in handsewn silk bags. Soon he was overwhelmed with orders for tea in bags. Many tea lovers, however, looked down their noses at tea bags, claiming that simmering loose leaves was the only proper way to brew tea. Others, however, enjoyed the convenience of teabags. Because the tea particles in the bags were small, the tea brewed faster. Today, most people agree that tea bags do make an acceptable cup of tea.

got its name from the Latin word for ginger, *zingebar*. By that time gingerbread had become so popular that French and German bakers formed their own guilds, giving them the exclusive right to make the bread. However, they were not allowed to bake gingerbread on Christmas or Easter. Later that law was overturned, and Christmas markets became the rage all throughout Europe, featuring bakers making fresh gingerbread in their stalls.

Gingerbread houses were launched into prominence in the nineteenth century with the publication of "Hansel and Gretel." Sometimes thought of as an old-fashioned cookie and sometimes thought of as an elaborate dessert, the two reputations of gingerbread are equally deserved. Gingerbread was once so precious that it was gilded and considered a treat fit for the king. In fact, a common saying was, "The gilding is off the gingerbread." Early Americans contributed to the countrified view of gingerbread, adapting the recipe to fit with available ingredients. New Englanders used maple syrup in place of sugar, and Southerners added molasses to their recipe.

The air broke into a mist with bells.

—ROBERT BROWNING

5

The Season of Giving

FOCUSING ON THE TRUE MEANING OF THE SEASON

*Christmas is a season of giving. Please come to my tea party
and let me share the gift of friendship with you.*

Most of our favorite Christmas stories and poems contain a not-so-small lesson about the importance of giving. In O. Henry's short story "The Gift of the Magi," a poor yet devoted husband and wife sacrifice their most prized possessions in order to give each other a meaningful gift on Christmas. Charles Dickens' short novel *A Christmas Carol* tells the tale of the miserly Ebenezer Scrooge, who, through seeing vignettes of his own life pass by—past, present, and future—discovers that the richest rewards are in giving. Even the humorous children's book *The Best Christmas Pageant Ever* contains an important message about how we should treat other people.

Unfortunately, today's emphasis on purchasing impressive and expensive presents for friends, family members, and coworkers often swings too far to the side of materialism.

What was originally intended as a joyous act that brought a smile to the heart of both giver and receiver has become a major cause of stress in some of our lives. That is not how it was meant to be. While it's wonderful to give what we can, we should definitely embrace the old adage that "it's the thought that counts."

Focus on the true meaning of the season with The Season of Giving tea party. It doesn't have to be fancy, nor does everything have to go perfectly according to schedule. There are elements of surprise and fun in flexibility. Invite your children's best friends to come over after school for tea, or ask a few families to join you for a party after the church Christmas pageant. You can invite people you are close to, but you can also add to the guest list someone you'd like to get to know better. Come together over simple food and an easy craft for the kids, and then engage in some good, rich visiting. Everyone will be renewed and refreshed by the time spent together.

Menu for The Season of Giving Tea Party

SWEET TEA SPREAD ON BROWN BREAD • CUCUMBER SANDWICHES
PUMPKIN PIE CAKE • SUGAR COOKIES

RECIPES

Sweet Tea Spread on Brown Bread

3 ounces soft cream cheese
Grated rind of 1 orange or lemon or
2 tablespoons orange, lemon, or ginger marmalade
⅛ teaspoon paprika

Combine all ingredients with hand mixer on low speed. Spread on your favorite brown bread.

Cucumber Sandwiches

Peel cucumbers and slice very thin. Sprinkle slices with salt and drain on paper towels. Spread white bread with unsalted butter and a thin layer of cream cheese. Layer cucumbers no more than ¼ inch high. Cut into desire shapes.

Pumpkin Pie Cake

Crust:
1 cup yellow cake mix
2 eggs
½ cup melted margarine

Filling:
1 29-ounce can pumpkin
½ cup white sugar
½ cup brown sugar
1 cup evaporated milk
1 tablespoon cinnamon
3 eggs

Topping:
½ cup margarine
½ cup sugar
1 cup yellow cake mix
Chopped pecans

Layer in 9 x 13 greased glass pan and bake at 350 degrees for 1 hour.

Sugar Cookies

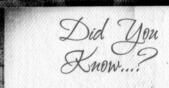

1 cup butter
2 cups sugar
4 eggs
2 teaspoons vanilla
5 cups flour
4 teaspoons baking powder

Cream butter and sugar. Add eggs and vanilla. Mix flour and baking powder into mixture. Chill. Roll and cut out seasonal shapes. Sprinkle with colored sugar. Bake at 350 degrees for approximately 12 minutes.

Did You Know...?

The Victorian rule of thumb for filling a Christmas stocking was "Something to eat, something to read, something to play with, and something they need!"

READYING THE ROOMS

The most basic of decorations can instantly transform your living room into a cozy Christmas tea room. A tree lit and hung with ornaments is a must, of course. Try to have some of your gifts wrapped in time for the party. A gathering of presents under the tree adds to the spirit of anticipation, and children will be drawn to the cheery packages. For a homespun feel, wrap this year's packages in plain brown paper and string, and then tie in just a bit of plaid ribbon and raffia. It's a very inexpensive yet attractive way to gift wrap.

In the olden days, the Christmas stocking—not the tree—was the main source of gifts for children. For farming families, a successful harvest meant a well-filled stocking. Edible treats such as gingerbread cookies, fruit-juice flavored hard candies, apples, and oranges bulged from stockings. Homemade toys such as dolls, wooden animals, and pebbles often found their way inside the stockings of little ones.

If you have children coming to visit for your Season of Giving tea party, ask them to bring a stocking from home to hang on the mantel. Sometime during the evening, have all the young ones retreat to another room to sing some carols, read a Christmas story, or eat a few freshly baked cookies (a quick sledding trip is the perfect diversion). While they're out

of the room, stuff a few oranges, candy canes, and cookies into the stockings. The gifts are simple, but the looks on the children's faces are guaranteed to warm the heart!

CUSTOMS OF CHRISTMAS

Most people today equate gift giving with Santa Claus but aren't aware that there is a special story about who Santa Claus really was. He was a dear Christian man named Nicholas, and we call him St. Nicholas. In his town lived many poor children who didn't have enough food, clothes, or toys. St. Nicholas used his own money to buy them what they needed. He didn't want the children to be embarrassed by his gifts, so he gave them secretly. St. Nick always gave in the spirit of helping and sharing, and his example reminds us that it's better to give than to receive.

You've probably heard of a holiday called Boxing Day but might not be familiar with the custom. Boxing Day falls on December 26 and is celebrated by the British. The tradition began in the Middle Ages when the churches opened their "alms boxe"—boxes filled with gifts or money that people had donated throughout the year. The contents of the alms box were distributed to the poor and needy on the day after Christmas. Today, Boxing Day gifts are also given to delivery workers and children who carry newspapers.

Prior to the Victorian era, gifts were generally exchanged on New Year's Day or Twelfth Night, the evening of Epiphany. The Victorians popularized the custom of giving gifts on Christmas Day, and today some people do a little opening on both days.

A Word About Tea

In 1904, visitors to the Louisiana Purchase Exposition in St. Louis sweltered in a heat wave and declined the hot brew offered by Indian tea growers. An Englishman named Richard Blechynden, who represented the tea growers, tried pouring the tea over ice in order to please his visitors. The result was iced tea, which now accounts for eighty percent of the tea consumed in the United States. If you live in a warm climate, iced tea might be your ideal Christmas beverage.

6

Afternoon Elegance

PAMPERING GUESTS WITH TRADITIONAL GOOD CHEER

Please come and join me for a proper afternoon tea in celebration of Christmas.

*I*f this Christmas you're longing to escape back to a time of romance and gentility, an era of propriety and luxury, consider putting on a traditional Victorian high tea. This is the tea party where you pull out all the stops, dress your home—and yourself—to the hilt, serve an abundance of delectable sweets, and pretend that you're back in the era of waltzes, petticoats, and horse-drawn carriages. It's a wonderful way to share the spirit of Christmas and express your love and appreciation for those who have made your year so special.

My tradition is to put on a formal tea every Christmas, and I love to go all out and create a celebration that everyone will remember long after the party is over.

An Afternoon Elegance tea party helps spread traditional good cheer and gives those you care about something to look forward to year after year. It's your love expressed in your preparations—the tea table standing at attention next to the Christmas tree, outfitted in snowy white linens and pearly china. A picture of joy.

A Word About Tea

To prepare your tea in the proper way, steep instead of boiling it. Tea leaves release their flavor in hot water, and the taste is more pleasant in the beverage that has been steeped. The hotter the water, the faster the tea will steep. Three to five minutes is sufficient steeping time for most teas.

Menu for an Afternoon Elegance Tea Party

TRADITIONAL TEA SANDWICHES • TRIFLE FIT FOR A QUEEN
SCONES WITH LEMON CURD

RECIPES

Traditional Tea Sandwiches

Afternoon tea sandwiches are made from very thinly sliced bread with crusts removed. Try these delicious ideas for filling:

- Thinly sliced chicken breast or smoked salmon with watercress and mayonnaise on white bread.
- Stilton cheese crumbled over apples on pumpernickel bread.
- Cream cheese mixed with chutney, a dash of curry, and lemon juice on white bread.
- Paper-thin slices of red radish on white bread with unsalted butter.
- Tomato slices sprinkled with freshly chopped basil on rye bread spread with mayonnaise.

Trifle Fit for a Queen

5 peaches, peeled and sliced
$2/3$ cup + 2 tablespoons peach schnapps
1 5 x 9 pound cake
Fresh berries for garnish
10 ladyfingers
1 recipe peach cream (recipe follows)
1 cup whipping cream
2 tablespoons sugar

Brush flat sides of ladyfingers with $1/3$ cup of peach schnapps and line the sides and bottom of a glass serving bowl with 8-10 cup capacity. Spoon half of the peach cream over the ladyfingers lining the bottom of the dish. Arrange half of the peaches on top of the peach cream. Slice cake lengthwise into $1/2$-inch slices and brush cake slices on both sides with ⅓ cup peach schnapps. Arrange half of the cake slices on top of peaches. Repeat layers of peach cream, peaches, and cake slices. Whip cream until medium-soft peaks form. Add sugar and 2 tablespoons schnapps and continue beating until blended. Spread cream mixture over the top of trifle and garnish with fresh berries. Wrap tightly with plastic wrap and refrigerate overnight.

Peach Cream

8 egg yolks
2¼ cups half-and-half
3 tablespoons peach schnapps
6 tablespoons sugar
4 teaspoons cornstarch

In a medium bowl, beat egg yolks until thickened. Gradually add sugar and beat until mixture is thick and lemon colored. Pour into a saucepan and beat in 2 cups half-and-half. Mix cornstarch with remaining half-and-half and beat into egg mixture. Cook over medium-low heat and stir constantly until mixture thickens (6-8 minutes). Do not let mixture boil. Remove from heat and stir in the peach schnapps. Cool to room temperature and then chill. Mixture will thicken more as it cools.

Lemon Curd

Grated peel of 4 lemons
Juice of 4 lemons (about 1 cup)
4 eggs, beaten
½ cup butter, cut into small pieces
2 cups sugar

In the top of a large double boiler, combine lemon peel, lemon juice, eggs, butter, and sugar. Place over simmering water and stir until sugar is dissolved. Continue to cook, stirring occasionally, until thickened and smooth. While still hot, pour into hot, sterilized ½-pint canning jars, leaving about ⅛ inch for headspace. Run a narrow spatula down between lemon curd and side of jar to release air. Top with sterilized lids; firmly screw on bands. Place in a draft-free area to cool and store in a cool, dry place. (I keep mine in the refrigerator.) Lemon curd doesn't keep indefinitely, so make only as much as you will use in a couple of weeks. Makes about 1 pint.

Readying the Rooms

As you prepare for the holidays, consider bringing the beauty of nature indoors as the Victorians did with ornately decorated trees, abundant fruit and floral displays, and swags of greens. Check at a local nursery to see what's available in your area during the wintertime, then choose a variety of flowers and greenery sure to bring visual pleasures as well as the delightful fragrance of the winter outdoors into the home. If you have pets or small children, limit your selection to nontoxic materials. Decorate mantels and staircase banisters with an array of fresh garlands, and pile armfuls of greenery on top of cabinets and bookcases. Twine some white lights through the greens to make an elegant display.

With their delightful color, scent, and texture, evergreens have long been a part of wintertime celebrations around the world. The hanging of greens, holly and ivy in particular, has long been a winter tradition in Great Britain, reminding them that spring and warmth were just around the corner. For primitive European tribes, branches hung above doorways promised good fortune and good health through the chilly months. The Romans exchanged evergreen branches with friends as tokens of good wishes.

Delight all of your guests' senses as they arrive at your Afternoon Elegance tea party. Once the greens have been placed throughout the house and the seasonal flowers have been put on display, put the fragrance of Christmas in the air. Bags of Christmas herbs, pinecones, twigs, and dried flowers will create a delicious scent throughout your home. For a quick and easy pick-me-up,

Did You Know...?

We have Anna, the Duchess of Bedford, to thank for the delightful tradition of a proper afternoon tea—tea served with miniature sandwiches, small cakes, and other such delicacies. In her day, the English people typically ate a large breakfast and a late dinner without much in between. By the middle of the afternoon, the Duchess always experienced a "sinking feeling," which she staved off by dining on tea, cakes, tarts, and biscuits at four o'clock in the afternoon. Thus was born the custom of taking afternoon tea.

sprinkle powdered cinnamon in an aluminum pie plate and let it warm slowly in your oven. A holiday baking smell will fill the air in no time!

Just a few more touches inside and out will complete the holiday ambiance–a Christmas doormat that brightens your front step; a fragrant wreath of evergreen branches; lots of little lights outdoors; jingle bells tied to the front door; and, most of all, a hearty welcome to your tea party.

A Proper Invitation to Tea

Victorian invitations to tea were works of art in themselves, extravagantly engraved on white paper. You don't have to go that far, but hand lettering (calligraphy, if you know it) looks very pretty and personal in this age of computers. Choose Christmas-themed stationery or design your own. You can add glitter, Christmas confetti, or other festive touches. The wording, however, should be simple and clear:

EMILIE BARNES
requests the pleasure of
your company for an
*Afternoon Elegance
Christmas Tea.*
Saturday, December 6
between four and six o'clock.
R.S.V.P.

CUSTOMS OF CHRISTMAS

If you'd like to put on a traditional tea with a capital "T," consider spreading your tea table with standard British fare from the 1700s and 1800s—capons and turkeys, geese and sirloins of beef, plum puddings and mincemeat pies. (Your guests will forgive you for leaving out the boar's head and the lamprey eel pie, I'm sure.)

The Scandinavians celebrated Christmas with a bevy of traditional foods—animal-shaped *julkuse* bread and *limpa*, a bread made with orange peel and molasses. In addition to the classic *lutfish*, a great variety of sweets were served—seven different kinds of cookies! A Christmas Eve rice pudding called *risgrynsgrot* hid a single almond. If you found the almond, luck and marriage were sure to soon follow.

Fanciful desserts hailed from Germany—*marzipan, lebkuchen, springerle, stolen*, and a mouthwatering collection of spiced cookies. In America, the Pennsylvania Germans made sure to eat their daily seven sweets and seven sours along with black walnut cake, fruit dumplings, macaroons, and a concoction of popped corn, nuts, and taffy syrup.

A Mexican Christmas tradition is a special hot chocolate, made with a Mexican chocolate which is composed of sugar, almond, and cinnamon. The drink is whipped with a wooden stick called a *molinillo* that is rolled back and forth in your hand.

Consider where your family comes from and the heritages of your guests. It's fun to bake these traditions right into your holiday celebration with a variety of customary treats.

There are few hours in life more agreeable than the hour dedicated to the ceremony known as afternoon tea.

—HENRY JAMES, *Portrait of a Lady*